THE PASSAGE TO PASSIVE INCOME

RAHAT KATOCH

ISBN 978-1-63974-436-7

Terms and Conditions

LEGAL NOTICE

RAHAT KATOCH

Foreword

Any income where the individual does not have to physically earn is called passive income.

This ofcourse is a very attractive way of earning an income and indeed those who are lucky enough to make a decent living this way are quite happy.

The Passage To Passive Income

Generate Truckloads Of Passive Income And Live The Four Hour Work Week

Contents

CHAPTER ONE

What Is Passive Income

There are currently some very popular and common ways to derive passive income. Writing a new melody or song or even a jingle and the selling it as a commercial property will garner some very lucrative passive income.

Opening a bank savings account, is another way which just by saving money get the individual some interest residual income though it is not that much and fluctuates often at the whim and fancy of the banking systems.

Learn the basics

Starting a multi level business is another way to generate passive income. These companies don't require the standard work of recruiting and selling product but becoming a financial product consultant is not only a good passive income source it is also a way to expand the client base.

For those with a little more money to spare, they can consider other type of investments which are likely to bring in the returns. Buying property and then letting it out helps the individual to pay for the loan thus not requiring any immediate financial commitment.

There are a lot of innovative ways to make money of the internet engine. One of the more popular tools include the creation of sell on line tools that require perhaps language changes.

On the more risky way of getting passive income would be to invest in various stocks and bonds.

CHAPTER TWO

Using Residual Income

After paying off all monthly commitments the money left over is known as residual income. This income can be of great help to an individual and is normally linked to the older more established income group.

This is also the way the banking industry calculates the probability of giving out a loan commitment to their clients. This is an income that also continues to give well past the time frame of the first initial payment.

Residual Income (RI)

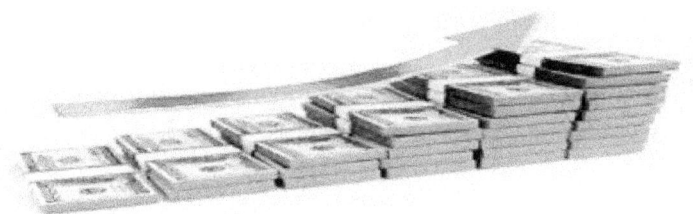

What's Left Over

There are many ways to try and earn residual income. Writing for instance is one way of adventuring into this realm of gaining residual income.

Becoming famous like perhaps as an actor or singer, where there are still payments coming in every time the work previously done is reused. When this is done for further entertainment modes, the said entertainer gets a residual income in the form of certain percentages form the original initial performance.

Earning residual income from real estate is perhaps one of the more popular styles of investment with this intention in mind. If done well this type of residual income is the most ideal and profitable.

Other much simpler ways of getting residual income would include starting a savings plan early on in age. Keeping to this diligently would help to ensure the comfortable retirement where residual income would be a great help.

The best types of residual income plans are normally where the individual had total autonomy over how, where and when the product is used.

CHAPTER THREE

Using Leveraged Income

This is perhaps among the most beneficial ways of creating the possibility of having a continuous income in a long term scenario. Using the leverage income style, the individual ears more money with much less effort simply because the profits made don't only come as a direct result of one's own efforts but also from the added sources of other people's efforts.

Utilizing

Ideally most people work towards trying to earn this style of income both in the short term and long term scenario. In its most basic terms, leverage income allows the individual to concentrate on other endeavors once the initial stages of setting up and getting a particular project started. This said project is then left to generate income with no need for anymore particular daily involvements.

Most people who are financially comfortable have ventured into this type of investment. Using a little time and effort to realize a project and then stepping back as the project eventually runs itself is indeed the perfect scenario. Thus this leverage style of earning power gives the individual the option to retire early and enjoy the fruits of his or her labor without the hassle of having to oversee the foray to be physically involved.

Besides the various investment arms that can be used to generate leveraged income, starting up a marketing company or business venture is also one of the more popular ways of generating this style of income. This of course requires a little hard work in the beginning but once the business is established then there will no longer be a need to be as completely involved as in the initial stages.

CHAPTER FOUR

Using Active Leveraged Income

Active leveraged income works on more or less the same principals of the normal leverage income format with one significant distinction. In this style the individual will be required to be more hands on and have a higher percentage of involvement in the initial stage and at some stagnated stage throughout the foray.

Therefore, building leverage into your business is essential.

Action

Being able to provide a service or product that "keeps on giving" on a large scale would be of course quite ideal, thus making a study of such a product or service may bring about some rather interesting and viable options.

Some of the simple options of active leveraged income would include providing one's services at workshop conferences and seminars. Also conducting training session for corporations is also beneficial as the material used would have already been designed as a basic format to be used over and over again with only a few adjustments being made every so often.

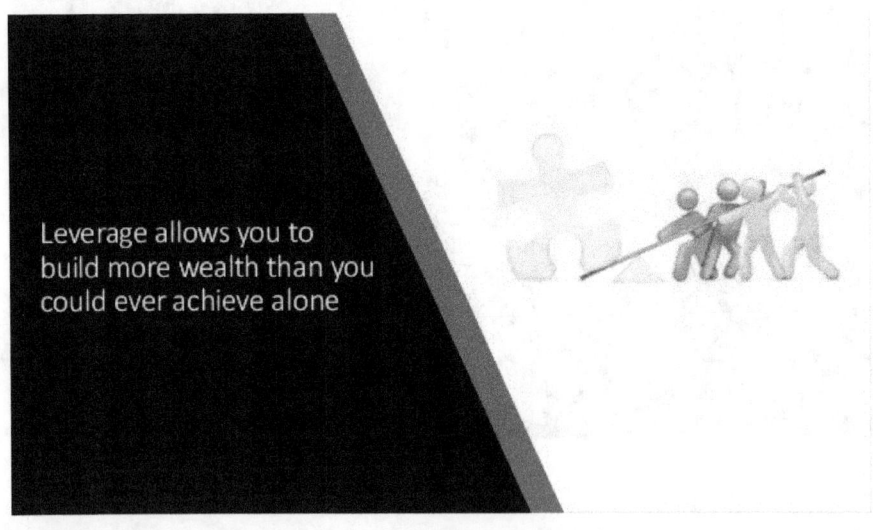

Leverage allows you to build more wealth than you could ever achieve alone

Designing good home study modules are also another very profitable way of garnering the leveraged income style of earning a comfortable living. This also requires an initial investment of time and effort which usually create the platform for continuous and profitable sources of income. Thus by doing so, it allows the individual to then be able to focus on other possible forays to further enhance the income base.

The more successful formulas used in the past just required the individual to focus on designing a product or service that would be continuously and consistently used and reused, thus creating the desired revenue that would eventually evolve into leveraged income.

CHAPTER FIVE

Using Internet Marketing

Internet marketing is also referred to by several other terms such as digital marketing, web marketing, online marketing, search marketing, and e marketing. All these have the similar marketing style with only a few minor difference but all have the main intention of making money. The future of your business depends on it.

The Net

This style of marketing is considered to be fairly broad and lucrative. This style may include services like creative and technical assistance, designing, development, advertising and sales. Internet marketing tool can provide the interactive customer engagement, a search engine provider for marketing purposes, a platform for ads, and many other possible earning tools.

The use of the internet marketing tool can provide for the one to one approach which is not always possible in the "real" world scenario. This approach though fairly broad and with no particular direction can be reached through the use of key words which are entered by the user in order to garner the required information or service.

Designing marketing tools which are supposed to appeal to specific interest groups is also done through the internet marketing route. This style created the platform for the connections to be made between a typical segment group and the product touted.

Niche marketing done through the internet marketing tool has its merits. The success of the style is very successful indeed and is certainly popular with those people who have limited time and interest to browse the internet. Thus this service provided is very beneficial to them and wide used too.

The advantages of creating an internet marketing business has it many advantages, ranging from the possible huge incomes derived to the leisure pace one can dictate. However nothing of course comes without some level of effort put in to see the success desired and being the most common tool of business now, it is well worth the effort to look into.

CHAPTER SIX

Using Network Marketing

It is a people person form of marketing, there is an actual need for people to go out and look for customers who may be interested in the products being sold. This method is used when it is deemed better than garnering any business through other methods like off line and on line marketing tools. Here the use of independent representatives is the key to the success rate of the business foray.

Networking

Recruitment drives are often conducted to try to get people to sign on to be agents or individual promoters for a company. Some of these companies follow the multi level marketing styles while others just need to identify potential distributors.

Using the network marketing to create residual income is another form of providing for a more comfortable living from a financial angle. This form of earning is done at the individual own pace and commitment. Basically the harder one works the better the chances will be to gain a higher residual income.

The individual also has the privilege of deciding who and when to conduct any business with. This is a very important aspect for some people who enjoy meeting and making new friends while at the same time gaining the advantage of an extra income source.

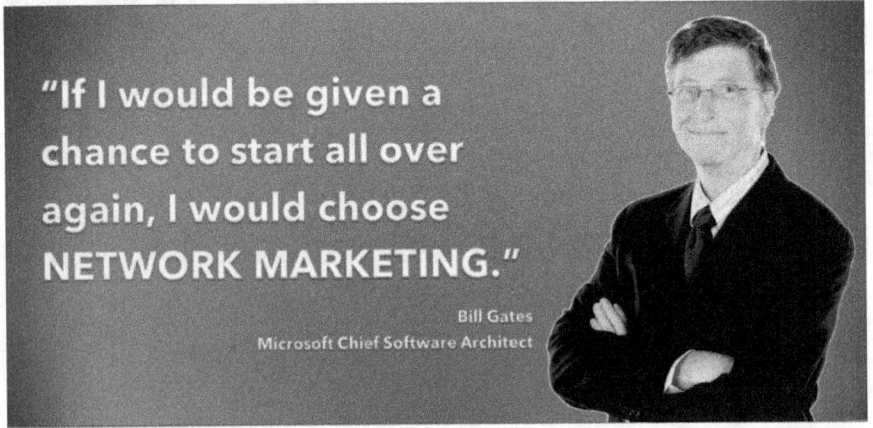

"If I would be given a chance to start all over again, I would choose NETWORK MARKETING."

Bill Gates
Microsoft Chief Software Architect

This method also usually involves very little monetary investment and neither does it involve a long term commitment. The reason most people opt to try their hand at network marketing is because of the very lucrative promise of a residual income prospect.

Seeing the success of others who have managed to achieve a comfortable financial status is a good bench mark to focus on in the pursuit of the individual's own ambitions for a good and healthy residual income. Another interesting thing to note is that there is no age limit to this kind of endeavor.

CHAPTER SEVEN

Using Real Estate

This is another form of creating residual income without having to be too confined to any particular style or commitment requirement. Buying real estate to create residual income is fast gaining popularity as the success rate and remunerations can be rather enticing.

Real Estate

Some of the "pull" factors include the ability to control the levels achieved in terms of income garnered. There are very rarely any quotas that are put in place or forced upon the agents.

However for some real estate agents that who are attached to certain companies there are various incentive programs that are put in place to help generate the drive to push the agents to higher achievement standards.

Creating one's own personal security with the residual income from selling real estate is also another attractive reason to venture into this endeavor. The income that is derived from this particular type of residual income is definitely worth the reason for working towards an early retirement plan.

In making the decision to venture into the real estate style of garnering residual income the sense of being able to have some control over one's own priorities is an advantage. This will also allow the individual to practice a sense of responsibility and commitment in order to see the success of his or her foray into real estate.

There are also some very good tax advantages in using real estate to garner a tidy residual income base. This can be reflected in the system that is currently used to encourage the active sale of real estate.

Thus by providing the necessary tax breaks the individual is more likely to work even harder to achieve a comfortable residual income target. Diversifying one's ability to garner residual income without having the hassle of having to set up a separate company or organization is a better option to consider.

CHAPTER EIGHT

Using Blogs

Using this method for the purpose of earning residual income is a need thing at the moment. For those who are internet savvy this is an excellent avenue to pursue in the venture of creating residual income for one's self.

Thought having a certain level of experience is somewhat necessary, it is not absolute as everyone has to start somewhere. Learning to use the best techniques available to create successful blogs will directly relate to the amount of residual income derived.

Web Logs

In order to be able to achieve a fairly lucrative residual income from blogging there must be a certain amount of commitment. The success of blogging depends largely on the individual's interest levels and ability to look for relevant information in order to ensure the blogs done are interesting and captivating.

Focusing on the promotional aspect of blogging will ensure the relevant amount of exposure needed to make the blog as frequently visited as possible. Promoting one's content on a social networking website and also leaving the relevant web page information will ensure the blog is well connected. This is also create the higher percentages required when there is more traffic generated via referral sites.

Featuring advertisements on the individual's blog will also provide a source of income as the individual is in the position to charge for the postings. This is only applicable if the traffic to the said blog site is a lot, thus there will be a lot of other people or companies willing to pay to be feature as adverts within the blog site, with the intention that it will in turn bring traffic to their sites too.

Getting other people to write interesting things that are then featured in the individual's own blog is a very good way to keep the blog interesting and diversified.

CHAPTER NINE

Setting Goals And Having A Plan

Plans and goals go hand in hand, without one the other is redundant. Having both these elements highly featured in one's life is the key to keeping focused on gaining better life conditions every step into the future

Suggestions

In most scenarios money play a big part in being the motivating factor that pushes the individual. The motivation levels of an individual are indeed what drives the endeavor to the success levels achieved.

As most people today are looking for easier ways to make money, the birth of many new endeavors are seem almost daily. More and more creative ways are being thought up with the main intention of making money as much and as quickly as possible.

Once an individual has decided on a goal, the next step would be to come up with a suitable plan to execute the goal successfully. Points like marketability, commitment levels, financial investments, man power are just a few things that need to be considered when drawing up the plans.

Taking the time to actually seriously consider the ambitions of the individual will help contribute to having a clearer picture of what the goals and plans should be. Indentifying this is most important to ensure the plan and goals are worked towards and finished successfully.

Knowing one's capabilities and being realistic when deciding the goals and plans is also one way of being wise and prudent. This will not only ensure the goal is achieved but will also keep the individual focus on achieving it quickly.

CHAPTER TEN

The Mindset Necessary For Passive Income

Those people who have successfully ventured into the passive income style of creating an income for themselves have been noted to have a very different mindset from the average individual.

What You Need

Generally the individual who chooses to provide residual incomes for themselves through the passive income style are people who are very focused. A strong positive mind set is almost a prerequisite in keeping the individual in track toward success.

Being hopeful is also another attribute needed for this kind of endeavor because this style of residual income does not have the pressure for not achieving a certain amount of business the individual has got to have all the necessary positive attributes to be able to push themselves to the next level.

People are normally driven by ambition and money and will go to almost any lengths to achieve both. In the pursuit to achieving the desired residual income through passive means the individual needs to be willing to try any types of endeavors.

Wrapping Up

There are many self starters that have chosen to venture into this type of earning arrears. Most of them already have the drive and the goal of being a success firmly in place and all they require is to be able to identify the relevant endeavor which will provide for what they desire.

They are always alert to any possible avenues that will allow them to create a healthy residual income scenario. Being always in the know will also ensure they are very aware of the possibilities available to them.

www.ingramcontent.com/pod-product-compliance
Lightning Source LLC
Chambersburg PA
CBHW061522180526
45171CB00001B/288